75164   B
                        824.4
Reghaby·   R4

Philosophy and freedom

Date Due

JA 2 5 '72	APR 3 0 2002		
NO 1 5 72			
DE 1 2 72			
MAY 2 4 7 pd.			
OCT 2 7 8			
FEB 12 '86			
JUN 2 5 87			
JUN 1 5 1990			
NOV. 12. 1991			
MAY 2 9 99			

CHABOT COLLEGE LIBRARY

25555 Hesperian Boulevard

Hayward, California 94545

PHILOSOPHY AND FREEDOM

PHILOSOPHY AND FREEDOM

by

HEYDAR REGHABY

PHILOSOPHICAL LIBRARY
NEW YORK

DEDICATION

DEDICATED to a most inspiring philosopher of freedom, my great friend and teacher, Dr. Hans-Joachim Lieber, Professor of Philosophy and Sociology at the Free University of Berlin.

Contents

I INTRODUCTION   9

II THE CONCEPT OF ACADEMIC FREEDOM   19
    What Is Academic Freedom?   20
    University as a Free Institution   23
    Internal Academic Freedom   25
    Faculty Beyond Administration   26
    Identity of the Faculty and the Student Body   28
    University and Society   29

III THE INTELLECTUAL REVOLUTION OF TODAY   33
    A New Social Power   34
    The Main Characteristics of the Intellectual
        Revolution   37

IV PHILOSOPHY OR RELIGION?   43
    Foundation of Religion   44
    Foundation of Philosophy   45
    Reason Replaces Faith   48
    Restoration of Human Reality   49
    Philosophy as Religion   53

V FREEDOM IN ART: A PROSPECTIVE IN AESTHETICS   55
    The Answer of Philosophy to the Question
        of Artistic Freedom   56
    Synthesis of Determinism and Freedom   62
    The Exceptional Case of the
        Exceptional Geniuses   66

VI LIFE AS CREATIVENESS   71

VII MAN AND THE ENDLESS UNIVERSE   79
    Index   89

I

Introduction

DURING THE FIVE YEARS of my teaching career I have found the subject "freedom" to be the most attractive melody to my students' ears. Of all topics suggested, all subjects considered, and all issues discussed, freedom seemed to be the key question. It was the first or the last, and to be more accurate the last and the first. It manifested itself as the central element of every problem or any solution. All patterns of thought seemed to start from it or to end with it! I was gradually led to a convincing conclusion: freedom is a concept of relativism which deals with all thoughts and all ideas. Even a determinist in his concept of determinism has an idea of freedom. In that he refutes the possibility of freedom, he implies its desirability.

Freedom may not often exist as a reality but it always exists as a desire. It is desired as an "idea" as a "concept," or as a "destiny." It is the most essential characteristic of life. It is life and it is idea. As an idea it is the most attractive manifestation of life demanding all domains of science, philosophy and art. And as life it is the most serious realization of idea in terms of existential relationships. Thus, the term "freedom" manifests at the same time the "idea" rooted in "life," and "life" elevated to "idea."

Freedom is a twofold pre-supposition of the idea of life and the life of idea!

Freedom as idea in general sense is a psychological product of "existential-confrontations": living mind confronting the external world constantly and continuously! It is in this continuous confrontation that freedom gains its meaningful reality and becomes a necessity. And only because of this confrontation freedom becomes a question. Man in his constant confrontation becomes a searcher; a searcher for freedom! And his search is as continuous as his life.

But man confronting the world means consciousness facing the physical reality. In this process of "facing the physical reality" we observe a twofold functional reflection: consciousness reflecting on "itself" and on the "other," and then on itself again; thus becoming self-conscious and demanding freedom.

From this standpoint the concept of freedom must be considered as a product of "consciousness" and a realization of "self." As the essential characteristic of the conscious life, it is conceived by the conscious man alone. Thus "consciousness" is the source of freedom, without it freedom is meaningless, unnecessary and irrelevant.

Consciousness is also the source of all methodical inquiries about "self" and the external "encompassing" the stream of inward and outward reflections. Consciousness searches for freedom and meanwhile develops its own essential method for this search. It produces philosophy. Thus, according to this consideration, philosophy is the main discipline and freedom the main object of consciousness.

Philosophy and freedom, while representing the main characteristics of consciousness, are subject to an essential relationship with one another. They are essentially interrelated, which means that their togetherness is not accidental, nor does it represent a linguistic phantasy, nor a baseless imagination of a teacher of philosophy. It is the application of a conceptual interrelationship which leads the two terms ultimately together: Philosophy and Freedom!

✓ ✓ ✓

The history of philosophy is an intellectual explanation of man's general history. It demonstrates a constant search for man's freedom, showing the direction of all sciences and arts, all modes and moves of man's mentality: a direction towards freedom. One does not have to be necessarily a Hegelian to see this direction and to call the stream of history a progress in the consciousness of freedom. Nor is one to be a Kantian to see the function of "a priori elements of the noumenal freedom" in man's general attitude. Nor must one be forced to follow existentialism to consider freedom as the main characteristic of manhood. The concept of freedom is the central concept of all philosophies at all times. Yet it is the modern philosophy which places its greatest emphasis upon this central concept of thinking and brings the term "freedom" to its most immediate neighborhood.

In this little book of essays, I am talking about this conceptual neighborhood. The historically advanced immediacy of such a conceptual togetherness shall explain the relationship of these various essays with different subject matters but with the same general aim of inquiry: freedom.

Philosophy searches for freedom in academic life, in man's social convictions, in art, in science and in philosophy itself! Philosophy forms a question and philosophy seeks the answer for it. Philosophy searches for freedom in life. In order to become a philosophy of freedom it has to become a philosophy of life first. Thus in this particular stage of history most of the philosophical inquiries are becoming existential and, at the same time, most of the existential problems have a tendency to become philosophical. Philosophy extends from individual contemplations to social revolutions. It is behind political movements, artistic products and scientific discoveries. Everywhere it is motivated by the vital questions of freedom.

In that "freedom" becomes a question, "philosophy" becomes a necessity. And freedom has constantly been a question. The problem of freedom has always been a life-relating
cause of philosophy. The conceptual relationship between
"freedom" and "philosophy" is only meaningful when it is
mediated by the concept "life." Considering that freedom is
to be interpreted in terms of life and life in terms of freedom,
philosophy's consideration of one would be impossible without the other. In other words: philosophy sees freedom
wherever it sees life, and it projects life whenever it projects
freedom.

⌁   ⌁   ⌁

Philosophy's projection of life is a projection of multiplicity. The following essays are only a selected few from
many problems of the combined subject "life-freedom." As
a concerned observer and as a member of the academic community, I have directed my first inquiry to the problem of
freedom in academic life.

Here the freedom of the thinking mind seems to be a
most important factor. The concept of academic freedom
seems to have been derived from a simple principle: freedom
to think! Freedom for the thinking mind which thinks about
freedom! This is the simplest and the most inclusive principle
from which an inquiry of academic freedom begins and to
which it returns.

Of immediate relation to this basic thesis are the social
implications considering the relationship of the "academy"
with the "society." As a consequence of such a relationship
the freedom of thought and its political-social obstacles develop into a dialectical opposition. It is first a case of the old
beliefs against the modern ideas. But it develops frequently
into a state of arms against thoughts. But the logic of history

would have to pronounce the triumph of the synthesis of freedom.

The demand for freedom as reflected upon the consciousness of the academic community is, in a true sense, a demand of the society itself. But the society as a whole in conceiving, presenting and executing this demand is always one step behind the academic community. The opposition between the two, the academic community and the society, is the problem of this "one step behind." It is not an opposition of essence but of distance! And such a distance is subject to a timely cancellation in dialectical fashion.

Yet the opposition as an existing duality continues! The "distance" is frequently cancelled and constantly re-established. The dialectic goes on. This dialectical continuity should explain the main cause of campus disturbances around the world to indicate "The Intellectual Revolution of Today."

One of the conceptual manifestations of this "distance duality" of the opposites is the duality of "philosophy" and "religion" which receives its full realization through a progressive course of historical developments. This developed duality leads the modern man to a consideration of the whole issue as the question: "Philosophy or Religion?"

Philosophy as a former subordinate of religion emancipates itself from its master to renounce all superimpositions of religion. Now the emancipated philosophy is free to become an independent Weltanschauung and to present ideologies.

Philosophy as ideology is a philosophy of social freedom, a freedom caused by the force of change as reform or revolution, a freedom from the status quo. While, however, the dialectical emancipation from the status quo implies a general change with all possible forcefulness, it includes everyone and excludes no one. It is collective.

According to the demand of the emancipating ideology

the negation of the status quo is a negation of all reactions. And this is by necessity collective. Here conservatism is an enemy to be destroyed but only for the sake of collectivism! In reality while an old problem is solved a new problem is formed: the problem of uniformity: the lost individuality!

This situation suggests one of many examples where social freedom stays on the way of individual liberty. Thus the opposition of the old and the new reshapes as a different source of duality: the duality of individualism and collectivism which implies a confrontation between existentialism and socialism.

"Freedom in Art" is a study of one of the aspects of this confrontation. The question of artistic freedom leads the observer to the old hostile camps of determinism and freedom. While none of the associates of either side is willing to see the other, the observer sees them both and is able to conclude that every side is a victim of onesidedness, and that the philosophical truth has at least two sides. Thus the aesthetical truth does not seem to express only the genius of the artist or merely the deterministic factors of the society, but both. It is not purely individual or only social, but individual-social. It is existential; a synthesis of determinism and freedom!

The element of freedom in this and in every other synthetic conclusion is however the dynamic element of revolt. A synthesis does not remain synthesis for all times. It changes. And the potential quality of this change is the impatient element of freedom: freedom in demand of conquest, man in demand of re-creating reality!

"Life as Creativeness" is a demonstration of this re-creation, it is to picture man in his constant attempt to overcome the influences of the environment and to conquer pain. Man in this perspective is the symbol of happy conquest, the dynamism of revolting freedom.

The revolting man in search for freedom does not know any limits. Death is the only occasion which puts an end to this search. Life as continuity of living means to him a continuity of search for freedom, a revolt against less freedom and a demand for more! Freedom as the most vital question of his life colors all his desires, stamps all his actions, and conditions all his thoughts! He is then a total revolt against all restrictions; political, social, economical, scientific, religious, natural or environmental. And he is against death which imposes an end upon his life.

Man, with Nietzsche's Zarathustra, demands that all "joy" should become eternal. And against this real impossibility, he becomes the tragic poet who overcomes and re-creates reality. Art helps him to escape the destructive waves of the surface and to search in the ocean depths for the stream of the "Eternal Recurrence"! And the Dionysian artist develops a concept of eternity from the concept of time. Thus he becomes a preserved being which disappears with one stream of existence and reappears with another. He returns eternally. Hence, the preserved energy also means the preserved man!

Against this notion of preservation which in a way considers "man" and "matter" (or energy) as essential identities, there have been several objections. Idealism is one of them.

Idealism which, in Platonic fashion, considers man as a matter of duality thus tracing his physical reality to the physical world, and his soul to a superior order of metaphysical nature, denies that man's everlastingness could have a material source. The objection of idealism is derived from knowing man as a conscious being and different from the unconscious nature. There is an obvious implication of freedom here: man who is superior to matter is free from it! But even this solution does not satisfy man's endless thirst for freedom. Man in the process of idealistic interpretation is freed from the chains of "matter" only to be captured by metaphysical "ideas"! The freedom of man according to idealism is not so much a matter of individual consciousness but a question of consciousness in a total and metaphysical sense!

The idea of freedom is, however, a characteristic of the conscious individuality. Hence freedom without individuality is a contradiction in concept. Idealism, in order to bring the individual to a mystical destiny of essential unity, must deny his individuality first. It is bound to overcome this existential reality. It has to overcome the infinite plurality of consciousness for the sake of an abstract unity.

But the plurality of consciousness is man's potential freedom. It indicates the substantial multiplicity of conscious individualities. In that the individuals are consciously different, they are consciously individuals and consequently in demand of independence and freedom.

✓ ✓ ✓

The concluding chapter "Man and the Endless Universe" is a final reflection on the subject freedom, a conclusion which leads back to the introduction. Our inquiry started with the individual man and shall end with him. We will ultimately come back to our primary thesis to conclude that man as individual in the state of social interrelationship, is the true self-consciousness and thus the main subject matter of freedom.

As compared to the external infinity of the senseless universe, man is the infinity of inwardness. He tries to know the universe which does not know him or even itself. He discovers rules and regulations governing the external realities which force it to their undisputed domination! He learns about the mechanical functions of the ignorant physical environment. But he, this man of consciousness, revolts against them to re-emphasize his independence. Mechanical laws of nature or of the society may influence but may not govern his inner-reality. He is free to follow them or to resist them.

In this sense it is not the degree of his success which determines his freedom but the degree of his self-consciousness, the strength of his will!

Truly considered, freedom has its essence in man's nature, in man's consciousness of freedom. Hence to be free primarily requires a reflection upon "knowledge" and a relation to the "will" for freedom. In order to *be* free, one must first know freedom and also want to be free! What follows next is the realization of this freedom, or in Hegelian language, the making of human history. Human history is the history of freedom in realization and the record of human struggle for freedom. And this is what philosophy sees.

II

The Concept of Academic Freedom

When a deed is done for Freedom,
through the broad earth's aching breast
Runs a thrill of joy prophetic,
trembling on from east to west . . .

—James Russell Lowell
(from "The Present Crisis")

THE QUESTION OF human freedom is the dominating question of human history. Every purposeful movement in history has been a movement for freedom: The freedom of something from something, or someone from someone.

History began with man's conscious struggle for freedom from confining forces of nature. As opposed to the history of nature, the history of man is the history of consciousness: a gradually but constantly developing awareness of freedom. Man's consciousness of freedom, however, was in reality his self-consciousness. As soon as he knew himself he understood himself as an essentially free being.

The philosophical definition of history as "progress in the consciousness of freedom"[1] has not only a metaphysical-his-

---

[1] Hegel, G. W. F., *Philosophie der Geschichte*, Sämtliche Werke II, Glockner Ausgabe, p. 46.

torical, but also, and especially, a historical-social significance. This is a key principle to the understanding of every major historical movement as a movement toward freedom. Renaissance, Reformation, Enlightenment, and all progressive social revolutions illustrate this point.

Every incident of progress was also an incident of freedom. It served as a historical progress in freedom to justify the historical freedom for progress.

Further, all essential movements of freedom were intellectual. Where then, if not in the intellectual domain of human life, has human freedom its origin? The immediate answer to this queston is the ultimate answer to the question of academic freedom.

What Is Academic Freedom?

The essence of academic freedom is freedom of mind, the first of all freedoms.

Reason is free. And mind is the essential instrument for reasoning. Since Reason is free, mind as the instrument for reasoning must also be free. The reason for the freedom of mind is therefore Reason.

The freedom of mind may find a further support from Descartes and his dualistic interpretation of mind and body. One major difference between mind and body is the essential freedom of mind. The mind remains free even if one's body is placed in prison. The prisoner cannot move but he can still think, his mind can still function and when it functions it functions freely. It can even think about the philosophy of freedom.

The philosophical assumption that mind functions freely is supplemented by the hypothesis that this free function of mind aims at the practical realization of this freedom. In language of philosophy, mind's ultimate objective is to actualize its potential freedom.

The realization of self-freedom as self-reflection, explains the identical relationship of "self" and "freedom." The self-awareness of mind, in other words, is at the same time an awareness of the fact that it is free.

Awareness is knowledge. It is a general knowledge of both one's self and the outside world. The mind studies itself and studies the world, and this is the endless process of the academic life. All sciences and arts, all humanities and histories, all discoveries and all explorations fall under this single headline: "academic life." Acknowledge the essential freedom of this life, realize the endless freedom of the nature of knowledge and you have a clear concept of academic freedom.

The word "academy" has a historical significance in our intellectual life. It is known to us from the ancient time as the name of the school established by Plato, a garden in Athens where Plato taught. For those thinking minds familiar with Plato's method of thinking, the word "academy" should be the reminder of an intellectual center where a free exchange of ideas in all fields of knowledge was joyfully exercised. Not only Plato's own followers but also his famous opponents, the Sophists, were present. What had brought all these various thinkers to one intellectual center was not a political force or an administrative authority, nor was it even a legislative act, but a general thirst for knowledge as knowledge. Plato's philosophy, despite some authoritarian tendencies, generally may be regarded as the first philosophy of academic freedom, as far as its general method of instruction is concerned. His famous dialogues illustrate this point. The parties to a dialogue were representatives of different and sometimes hostile viewpoints who had nevertheless gathered around a single table to search "truth." The discovered truth on each issue was not the arbitrary command of any single mind, but the free conviction of many. Plato, even when he established his own desired conclusions, discussed in full detail the opinion of his opponents. And his writings are the living documents of those detailed discussions.

The term "academy" also in modern times inherits its ancient application. The legacy becomes still more obvious when the adjective "academic" modifies its inseparable noun: "Freedom."

Today we call the most advanced centers of our intellectual life "universities." As an advanced educational institution a university is a center where all ideas of scientific, social, and cultural importance should meet.

The concept of "academic freedom" in this particular perspective means the freedom of scholars and searchers of knowledge within the institution. Since such an institution is a most advanced academy, it must also enjoy a most advanced degree of academic freedom.

A university is a unity but not a totality. It may be based upon a unitary educational system but not a total educational system. A unity of different educational systems is the logical expression of their variety. It is a unitary light which dissolves itself into various colors of the rainbow, and various colors of a rainbow integrate into one essential color; the color of colors which is the color of truth.

But the color of truth contains many colors. It is not red, green, or yellow. It is a blending of red, green, yellow, violet and all the others.

Pursuing the truth is, therefore, pursuing its variations. And this is the function of a free academy.

As a university president said:

"Remember that on a university campus all types of educational experiences are necessary and anything of educational value must not be denied to the students."[2]

Any elimination or limitation of the variety of educa-

---

[2] *Oklahoma Daily*, October 26, 1967.

tional experience means elimination or limitation of the most essential elements of knowledge: its generality and its freedom. It is like looking at a rainbow from which some colors have been removed.

University as a Free Institution

By the same token that freedom is the basic characteristic of "mind" without which mind would have no self-consciousness, a university without academic freedom would be without its essential self-identity. In other words a university is no university unless it enjoys academic freedom. And how does a university enjoy academic freedom?

In order to answer this question we have to reflect upon the basic definition of a university, first.

The term university as *universitas* was an educational product of the Middle Ages. It was a description of the plurality of the educational fields within an institutional unity. Universitas as a general term was applied to stress the generality of knowledge as a knowledge of generality. And that represented the timely fusion of the Christian and Germanic ideas, despite their essential contradiction with the traditional Greek philosophy. The basic inclusion of theology in this generality, however, did not mean the acceptance of the demanding influence of the Church. The universitas decisively opposed and fought any intervention of church or state.

Professor Gustav Mueller in his book *Education Limited* explores this institutionalized universality of knowledge as the free foundation of universitas and concludes that:

The freedom and independence of the university from local municipalities, churches, and territorial princes was in line with the Germanic freedom of guilds or corporations administering their own laws. Politically this freedom was gained by the poverty of the universities: if their liberty was threatened they simply disbanded; they had no "Plants" in as much as they used churches and monasteries for quarters.[3]

The historical conception of universitas, with its gradually developing notion of generality, provides us with a basic definition of the university today. One may call a university the institution of higher education which includes all theoretical and practical aspects of knowledge. It is a substantially combined institution of those who learn and those who teach. Take away either of the two elements and you have no university.

The advanced process of teaching and learning cannot be only concerned with the academic status quo, but it must also consider the academic future as the future of the academy. This process, as a becoming process, has to deal with what is becoming knowledge. Thus it has to look forward and to go beyond the existing academic situation both socially and scientifically. It has to advance and it has to advance with time and faster than time. In reality it is the advancement of time itself.

The advancement of time means time surpassing time, ideas succeeding ideas, convictions replacing convictions, and thoughts overcoming thoughts. And this is what progress means.

The intellectual process of becoming as the spirit of time must overcome time and all its social, religious and political prejudices. It has to challenge and to eliminate all obstacles of the future prior to the future. It must pave the way. And since it is freedom for the future, it must be free to act presently.

A university is an intellectual center where the academic process to the future must find its realization, and that needs academic freedom both externally and internally.

---

3 Mueller, Gustav, *Education Limited,* 1949, University of Oklahoma Press, p. 126.

A university is externally free when it can function independently of local pressures and all political, economic and religious influences. A university, and especially a state university, should be a symbolic representation of the general freedom of the state. It is the mind of the state which must function freely if it is to function at all. It should not follow any party line or any line which makes it a party. A free institution represents all parties without being representative of any party in particular. As the brain of the society it is the party of progress. And, for that matter, it must be free, free of all censorships and controls. If you are financing to build a university to censor ideas, you are not building a university but a prison. And you are building the worst kind of prison: a prison of mind.

Censoring a university means trying to imprison innocent minds, and this is far worse than imprisoning bodies of innocent men. I don't hesitate to call this a crime of highest degree. And if you claim a social justification for your act, it is still a social justification for social injustice, and therefore no justification at all.

Internal Academic Freedom

The second aspect of academic freedom is the internal aspect which is no less demanding than the external. Here I would like to quote Dr. Robert MacIver, a Columbia University professor and the author of *Academic Freedom in Our Time*:

> Have we academic freedom when the academy runs its own affairs without outside interference? An academy is a corporate body, directed by a governing board. Is it then the freedom of the governing board? But suppose this board decided how and what the faculty members should teach? Obviously that would be a violation of what is always meant by academic

freedom. True, it means the freedom of the academy, but it refers to the intellectual life of the academy. For that is what gives it its character, its being. This intellectual life consists in the activities of a faculty, including in the first place their relations to the students. It is an educational freedom that is at issue. The academy is free when the scholars who make it are free. And the academy is free when its governing board is free to protect and to advance this freedom.[4]

This statement deals with three distinct principles:

1. The academic freedom has direct reference to the intellectual life of the academy.
2. The intellectual life of the academy consists in the activities of the faculty as related to the student body.
3. The freedom of the academy requires that the administration protect the freedom of its scholars.

These principles would lead us to two basic consequences, upon which a functional academic freedom must operate: The supremacy of the faculty as compared to the administration and the essential identity of the faculty with the student body.

Faculty Beyond Administration

The logic of the supremacy of the faculty is the necessary outcome of the objective of the educational institution.

If the objective of an institution is to promote knowledge and to educate interested minds and finally to elevate the intellectual life of mankind, educators and scholars are the ones to receive full credit for it. This means academic freedom for action!

---

[4] MacIver, Robert M., *Academic Freedom in Our Time*, Columbia University Press, 1955, p. 3.

Unless this supremacy is acknowledged and respected, an academic institution is not free, and still more, it is neither academic nor an institution. The necessary elements of an academic institution are (1) academic standards, (2) institutionality and (3) freedom. If any of the three elements should be eliminated the academic-institution would degenerate into a private club, a church or a business.

The academic standards are the immediate expression of the dignity of the scholars and have a direct relationship to its growth or decline. Scholars are the leaders of academic freedom, and the only ones who can give a university the characteristics of an institution. They are supreme, therefore, also with respect to the idea of the institutionalization of the academy.

The absence of this supremacy leads to administrative dictatorship, and the rise of administrative dictatorship, if it is that of a single man or a group, would indicate the end of the academic life of the institution.

Many great universities of the world have eliminated this danger of dictatorship (1) by giving the university an academic leadership and by selecting the president from the true scholars, and (2) by making the scholar president responsible to the faculty as the supreme organ of the institution. As the consequence of this system, the university becomes both internally and externally free. As an independent organ it rejects all political, religious, financial and personal influences. This way the university avoids being a Marxist, a capitalist, an atheist, a religious or any sort of particular or ideological institution.

The supremacy of the scholarly body therefore puts the theory of academic freedom into action and develops a philosophy of freedom into a functional freedom in a modern sense. An academic leadership can best keep the institution free.

Identity of the Faculty and
the Student Body

The student body is the largest functioning organ of a university. It relates to the faculty on the basis of essential identity.

Teaching and learning are two united interchangeable efforts for a single purpose, a single process which indicates a duality of functions but a unity of aims.

Faculty and student body which are closely associated and essentially related have a common cause to defend and a common enemy to fear. Their common cause is a joint defense of academic freedom. In any case if they suffer, they suffer together and if they succeed, again, they succeed together. They may face together the pressure of the administration, if the administration should appear to function against the common interest.

If such a sad possibility should become a reality; if the freedom of either faculty or student body is challenged, both student body and faculty are endangered.

For concrete examples I can refer to the joint faculty-student strike of the Catholic University, April 1967, against the administration of that institution. Students and teachers were fighting side by side against a campus tyranny. The case was one of academic freedom. A professor who had made a brief statement in relation to the birth control problem, had been unjustly discharged. Not only his colleagues as his friends, not only his students as his students, but the whole student body and the whole faculty got together for a joint strike. The outcome was clear, the administration gave in and reinstated the professor.

Another example of this unity of the faculty and students

was shown recently by Columbia University. There, the powerful members of a supreme faculty stood up to defend the rights of the students and to stop the administration from revealing the students' records to external sources including the armed forces of the country. And this like many others was a successful case.

University and Society

The internal threat to academic freedom could be reduced or totally eliminated:

(1) When the supreme independence of the faculty is practically established and acknowledged.

(2) When the student body shares to some extent the governing power of the university with faculty and administration, and

(3) When the leadership of the university is entrusted to the hands of a president who has the full support of both faculty and students.

In this most desirable stage of internal harmony, a university is a unity. The administrators as allies of the scholars are scholars themselves. They can prove to be the best supplement to the faculty-student unity. Their leadership may be a sincere leadership acceptable to every sincere citizen of their institution. They are defended by the academy as long as they defend the academy.

In such a happy situation the problem of academic freedom is only an external problem. Thus the dialectical tension between scholars and administrators becomes a dialectical tension between university and society.

Acknowledging that the basic principle of academic freedom was the freedom of mind, and noticing that the function of mind was primarily the realization of its own freedom, we were led to conclude that the function of an academic institution is primarily the realization of academic freedom. It is inevitable that consciousness of freedom would develop with and through academic organizations. It is the "spirit of time" which indicates the inevitability of this awareness, this self reflection and this self consciousness. It is a timely determination which develops the consciousness of freedom, it is history. As history develops, the history of the academic institution develops with it. And this is intellectual progress as opposed to the outdated regulations and anomalies which exist in the present but belong to the past.

The self-knowledge of the academy is the consciousness of the intellectual life whenever it is challenged by the non-scholars. There was a time when the battle between scholars and non-scholars was most often won by non-scholars (the time of the Dark Ages and of Galileo, for example), which inevitably but gradually gave way to emancipation and then domination by scholars.

Tensions between an educational institution and the reactionary forces of society which try to stifle it need a dialectical explanation. On one side we have the center of progress, and on the other side seeds of decay. One side represents free movement of Reason, another side the rigid dogma of Faith! One side demands a decisive emancipation from the surviving censorships of the Middle Ages, another side insists in imposing these censorships upon the minds of the space age! One party is the courageous forerunner of the future, another party is the blind defender of the past. The first one tries to emancipate itself from the second, and the second one insists in keeping the first one its slave. The first party is the party of potential freedom and the second one is the party of actual negation of freedom.

What is the outcome of this long-lasting struggle of intensive tension, of this perpetual contradiction? A satisfactory answer may be given by Hegel and his analogy of Master and Slave.[5]

This philosophical demonstration shows how a self conscious individual, an individual who knows himself as an independent being, will be opposed by a second independent individual functioning as the negation of the first. The claim of both is the claim of independence and their Right is the Right for recognition of this independence. This way one self-consciousness opposes another self-consciousness and the outcome of this conflict is the temporary triumph of one over the other. One becomes master, the other his slave.

One example for this temporary triumph may be given as the forceful victory of theology over science in the Middle Ages. That was, however, not the end but only the end of the beginning.

To the dominating party, the party which is temporarily dominated is a "thing," an "object," a "subject of command" or a "slave." The slave, however, who is essentially a self-consciousness, cannot become essentially a slave. He is but only formally a slave. The longer the period of this formal slavery, the deeper the consciousness of the individual for freedom.

It is the perfection of this consciousness of freedom which, as a self-consciousness, explains the potential freedom of the slave. The next step is the step from potentiality to actuality. The slave who is potentially free becomes actually free.

The fight of the two begins again, but this time it leads to a domination of the dominated, or to a formal freedom from a formal slavery. This can be also the case of an academy which however essentially free, might be forced to a formal slavery. This has been the case of many universities under totalitarian governments. It may also be the case of democracy if a democracy attempts to tyrannize knowledge. Such a

---

[5] Hegel, *Phenomenologie des Geistes,* Meiner Verlag, Hamburg 1952, p. 143.

democracy would indeed be less than a tyranny. A true democracy can only grow in a democracy of knowledge, in a freedom of ideas and in a respectful relation to the academy where the soul of knowledge is the soul of liberty. A social freedom can never exist without an academic freedom.

If non-academic minds of a community succeed in once violating the freedom of an academy, they do not succeed in violating it forever. The necessity of academic freedom is a historical necessity. You can fight it but you cannot stop it.

The academy liberates itself by liberating the society which challenges its own liberty. Liberating the society means educating the society. It marches forwards while dragging its opponent with it. The society may still fight the academy, yet it has to follow it.

The academy grows and with it the number of its allies within the society. The enlightened forces of the society transfer gradually to the academy. Then as new forces of the academy they come back to the society again. This time, however, they come to conquer the society. And they conquer the society. They come back to change decisively. And they change decisively. This is truly observed a change of conquest and a conquest of change. It is the final victory of academic freedom.

III

The Intellectual Revolution of Today

"WE LIVE IN THE TWILIGHT of intellectual transition" wrote John Dewey in an essay of 1910. The significance of this philosophical statement was not probably understood then, but future developments made it a philosophy of the future. The whole 20th Century so far seems to be a century of transition. And this is a universal reality: Religion is being replaced by ideology, churches are diminishing by number and schools are increasing rapidly, education is being engaged in its most decisive battle against ignorance, self-determination of the Wilsonian school is finding its true meaning through liberal movements of independence. Colonialism has died and the new Colonialism is also dying. The surviving elements of the past centuries are losing their last stubborn strongholds against a movement of intellectual revolution. And this is a predicted reality which shows itself here and there, inside and outside of the U.S.

America is experiencing an intellectual revolution, a revolution national in function and international in character. This is an obvious manifestation of a social change which is bound to express itself also politically.

A living society is a changing society, change demanded by time and directed by timely progress. And the present intellectual revolution in America is an expression of the demand of time. It centers in the heart of the academic community and forms a challenge to the social and political status quo. The academic community, therefore, which is a functional social power, is now establishing itself as a social class, a class with universal slogan, universal aim and universal character: a universal class! Since the question of 'universality' is a question of the present time, this universal class is the class of the time, a determination of the present which itself determines the future.

A New Social Power

The universal class of the intellectual revolution in America and elsewhere is not only a social hypothesis, as some non-realistic "realists" want to believe, but a sociological reality: an existing factor in process of expression, expansion and determination. It is the basic factor of the academic life which is the most self-conscious, self-reflective and the most progressive phase of the life of the society. It is the consciousness of the society itself. It has not been a simple development from campus to campus, coast to coast, but also from country to country, and continent to continent. The question of the existence of such a factor, whose main objective is peace, freedom and self-determination, is not a blind question of desirability but a conscious question of actuality. It actually exists.

The newly developing social factor of universality may be called the "intellectual proletariat." And this shall be considered as a correction of the plain orthodox phrase "proletariat" known as the class of industrial revolution. Contrary to Marxism, the most conscious elements of this social transition are not workers or peasants, but the intellectuals. While a "Bible Belt" is fastened upon the most modernized farm territories, and while the majority of workers are the loyal students of the "Sunday Schools," the academic communities are fighting for freedom and progress against the status quo. And this is where the hypothesis of the duality of community and academy becomes a reality. And it is also here that education as liberation becomes a meaningful thesis.

A nine-month teaching experience at the University of Oklahoma led me to see the meaningfulness of this thesis. While I was preparing a speech on academic freedom to defend the independence of this University against the political interferences of the State, I was warned by some silent sufferers about the "consequences." I was told that this speech would place my name on the black list. In my opening remarks in the speech, I referred to this subject and concluded: "If a speech on academic freedom should lead to my becoming black-listed, I prefer to make the speech and to be black-listed!"

Before the end of the academic year a federal officer was brought to my office to revoke my visa and to give me 30 days to leave the country. I was told that I had violated the laws of the United States by teaching at this University. And the man who brought the federal officer to my office was a close assistant of the ex-president of Oklahoma University.

The reaction of the student-body and the faculty to my academic freedom-speech, however, was totally different. Here the thesis "education as liberation" was received, acknowledged and glorified. And here I saw my philosophy in action. I called Oklahoma a part of the changing world which is bound to change with the world. And it will be changed by the Oklahomans and by the devoted intellectuals and students whom I called: "the Army of Progress."

The intellectual army of progress is a sociological phenomenology of human consciousness which in this country and elsewhere is demanding a re-valuation of the existing values. The international student unrest is a demonstration of this demand and the United States is no exception. Also in this country, an intellectual revolution is taking place, a revolution of transition establishing itself as a force of negation. The question is: how prepared are the political machineries of the present to accept this growing force of negation as a social factor? Is there any place within the two-party system for this social force at all? And if so, who wins this new social power of the intellectuals? Which party is willing to follow the command of the present time in order to command the future?

A departure from the social and political status quo seems to be inevitable. The two-party system itself is a manifestation of this inevitability. The relation of the two parties should reflect the true relation of the social forces which they are supposed to represent. The parties are two because there are two essentially different categories of forces and interests within the society which are in constant opposition. The relationship of the two parties should therefore be a relation of the opposites or a dialectical relationship.

It is internationally known, however, that the Republican and Democratic parties in the U.S. have no real differences, and that the Democratic party does not serve as the social antithesis of the Republican organization. Foreign policy for example is said to be one unchangeable policy of intervention. The so-called Eisenhower Doctrine of 1956 was applied by the Johnson Administration in the Dominican Republic and Vietnam. The conception of "self-determination" therefore has become a joint misconception by both parties.

This sameness applies to the internal affairs just as well. The Democratic approach towards the minority and racial problems has no basic difference from that of the Republican approach.

Now the newly developing universal class of the intellectuals is itself a reason for a challenge against this "sameness." It is a social force to fill a vacuum, it is a power to become the power of opposition, it is a thesis to establish an antithesis. It can establish an antithesis with or without the Democratic party. And this is why the Democratic party now has a choice. It has a choice to join the opposition, to break its identical relationship with the Republicans and to become identical with the movement toward peace and progress.

The Main Characteristics of the Intellectual Revolution

The nature of today's intellectual movement may be known through five major characteristics:

1. It is radical and revolutionary
2. It is universal
3. It is objective
4. It is independent
5. It searches for universal freedom

I. *Why is it radical?*

The student movement, as a force of intellectual transition, is known as a radical opposition to the status quo. It is a positive movement in whose Weltanschauung, the principle of function is the principle of negation. It is the revolutionary nihilism of today which is trying to determine the values of tomorrow. In this sense the movement of negation becomes ultimately and inevitably positive.

This negation, as a force of destructive dynamism, is the inborn negation of the conservative institutions of the past and present. It grew with the growing militarism of our century. It is an intellectual movement of opposition which is fighting arms without arms. The intensity of the military dominations is the precise causation for the intensity of the intellectual opposition. And this is why the student unrest is radical.

II. *Why is it universal?*

The questions are asked frequently: why the students of one country demonstrate for or against another country? Why do French, British, German and Japanese students engage themselves in protest marches against the U.S.? Why these same student radicals condemn at the same time the aggressive moves of the Soviet Union, while they are not immediately affected by either? What makes them cross the border of national concern to fight, as hard as they can, for foreign victims whom they don't even know? Why the South-Americans, Americans, Europeans, Africans and Asians follow more or less the same principle of student opposition with similar slogans, and in a unified manner?

The answer to all these many questions can be given in one single sentence: the internationalization of aggression invokes an internationalization of opposition!

That the academic conscience is the conscience of humanity is an argument which needs no *a priori* principle of justification. It is a self-justifying reality which is sociologically understandable and historically observable. Here our argument is our proof.

The history of the 20th Century is the history of military dominations and social revolutions. The latter are not only the answer to, but also the phenomenological necessities of the former. The internationalization of the intellectual opposition therefore is a parallel development to the internationalization of military alliances of the present time. The first one is a function of crossing national borders to suppress a nationality, the second one is an action of crossing the same border to stop that function. The first one has weapons, the second one conscience. The first one relies on the dominative tradition of the past, the second one on the imaginative aspiration of the future. And the present is the front of this confrontation. It is now that the battle of the universal intelligentsia takes place. There is only one way out and that is the way to the future.

III. *Why is it objective?*

This movement on the way to the future is being presently criticized by two opposite military camps on the basis of false but purposeful accusations. The leaders of Russian-controlled countries condemn many European student movements, be it in Hungary, in Czechoslovakia or in East Germany, as a consequence of the Western conspiracy and stamp them immediately as a "Made in U.S.A." product! On the other hand, the officials of the NATO consider every student peace demonstration against the U.S. policy in Vietnam as a demonstration of Reds!

Both parties of this illogical black-or-white judgment know, however, that these accusations contain more propaganda than truth! Any experience with observation shows that the same students who demonstrated against the war in Vietnam, condemned also the Russian invasion of Czechoslovakia by signature and rallies of protest.

The truth is that the intellectual movement of today is against any military aggression from any side. This is what we call an objectivity of action. It is an elevating battle of principle which surpasses the aggressive policies of both blocs, fights them both and surrenders to none of them! It is not American or Russian, French or German, Chinese or Indian, Asian or African. It is all and it is none.

IV. *Why is it independent?*

A subjective judgment is the unavoidable consequence of any one-sided consideration. A judgment is subjective as long as one remains the blinker-wearing observer of only one side and is not willing or able to see the other! But the objective truth has many sides. In Hegelian language: "das Whare ist das Ganze"; truth is the whole.

All political and social forces of domination are powers of one-sidedness and any exclusive judgment from a single side is subjective! Every side presents and defends an interest of its own domination.

But there must be a party with no self-interest of domination to understand and to exercise objectivity, there must be a party which is beyond all parties and itself no party, concerned with all interests and itself showing no self-interest, a party of devotion and moral idealism in the true sense. This is the party of the independent Intelligentsia of today which proposes ideas against arms and liberation against domination.

V. *It Searches for universal freedom*

The universal class of the independent Intelligentsia has one basic aim: universal freedom! Since the threats and challenges to this freedom are also universal, the fight for this period of transition is a fight on many fronts. It is not a movement from the East to the West, against the West or the East, but a demonstration from all sides against all aspects of oppression.

Hence the student unrest has far more than a few motives. Perhaps the clearest example concerning the multiplicity of student's interest to fight against all variations of oppression is the Free University of Berlin.

The establishment of this university itself was the predictable consequence of the old university of Berlin, located in the Russian Sector. The Free University was founded in 1951 on the grounds of demands for academic freedom.

Ever since its establishment the Free University has been a center of intellectual opposition not only against the local authorities but also against international events of oppression as well. Here are only a few examples of these oppositions:

Building of the Berlin Wall in 1963 by the East German

Government, invasion of Hungary in 1956, the invasion of the Dominican Republic by the American forces in 1966, the growing escalation of the war in Vietnam, the visit of the King of Iran to Berlin in 1967 and the aggression of the Red Army with reference to Czechoslovakia in the fall of 1968.

The visit of the Iranian king provided the students of Berlin with a most successful opposition. After a student demonstrator was shot to death by a secret service policeman, the students, through a continuous strike and unrest, succeeded in forcing the mayor of Berlin to resign and the City Senate to dissolve itself and pave the way for new elections. The example of the German Students or that of the French (May, 1968) or others, are not given here to defend their claimed justification nor is it to overlook some of the ill-founded causes of "rioting for rioting" which had led to indefinite interruption of educational process. The purpose is to show the existence of the general intellectual movement as an effective social international force.

So far the effectiveness of this developing force has been denied by (a) the international political monopolies, (b) by the half-conscious and care-free citizens of the world, and (c) by those pessimistic opportunists who are the indifferent worshipers of "power," who do not see that power can also be resisted. Yet an intellectual revolution is taking place everywhere and is effectively negating all powers of domination and destruction.

The obvious aspiration of a Third World is a blossoming effect of this constructive negation. Today this may not be supplemented by adequate functional power, but there is always a tomorrow. History has frequently shown powers in transition, powers in growth and powers in decline.

Despite the transitory nature of power, everlasting is the idea of freedom which has never left the human consciousness and never let man stop trying. All masters have lost their domination. Even God is losing his crown to man.

IV

Philosophy or Religion?

THE MODERN AGE is the age of growing ideology and diminishing theology. As opposed to the past, when religion was considered to be a foundation of "spiritual" conviction and therefore a type of ideology, today ideology as philosophical conviction is a type of religion.

This historical transformation of religion to Weltanschauung of philosophy is, in a true sense, an elevation of the "spiritual" moment of human life to that of intellectual. The objective demonstration of this intellectual elevation is, socially speaking, the change of religious wars into ideological revolutions. And this began with the French Revolution of 1789.

Such a change was a consequent domination of faith by reason. It was inevitable. And history was a demonstration of this inevitability; a demonstration but a long and complicated one. It was meanwhile a demonstration of a prolonged conflict; the conflict between reason and faith, which in reality was experimental in the conflict of religion and philosophy.

History shows that the development of the human mind was the development of this conflict. At the very beginning religion as myth was undoubtedly a matter of historical priority, it was established before philosophy as philosophy came into the picture. Then the two were together; their togetherness, however, could not cover their essential contradiction. And finally we witness the separation of the two, due to the growing demand of philosophy for independence.

The demonstration of the conflict begins with the manifestation of undisputed religion and ends with the growth of unchallenged philosophy. The question of "philosophy and religion" and that of "philosophy of religion," becomes a question of "philosophy or religion." At this stage of development, religion which was a matter of historical priority is dominated by philosophy which claims to be a matter of logical superiority.

Foundation of Religion

Religion as a historical production has a prehistorical origin. It belongs to the most unknown period of human life. The period of mythological development signified a development of this unknown phenomenon to a half-known phenomenon.

The psychological motive of religion must have been a feeling of inadequacy towards nature, and a desperate attitude towards death, sickness and every natural disaster which proved to man that he was weak and limited.

Man who felt inadequate to fight nature worshiped nature. He considered himself as a "thing" below nature and wished to reach this "beyond" by going beyond himself, to become a part of the powerful "beyond" by resigning his inadequate reality.

Not reaching the security he had hoped to reach by worshipping nature, he now thought of worshipping something beyond nature. A supernatural power was considered as a protector of man against nature and man's natural inadequacy. His fear of nature became a supernatural hope. This fear and hope as a combined consequence of man's inadequacy was the principal psychological foundation of religion.

Foundation of Philosophy

In the depth of the psychological state of dependence, a desire for independence was growing. And this growth was at the same time a growth of man's knowledge about himself, a knowledge which did not quite approve of his absolute submission to an external power.

The disapproving knowledge was truly speaking, a thought of being which meanwhile indicated the being of thought. And this was the first foundation of philosophy.

If the total submission of mankind to nature and the supernatural was the origin of his religion, this partial negation of this submission was the origin of his philosophy. Philosophy therefore is the inborn negation of religion. It grows as human's knowledge of himself grows. And this is the basic demonstration of the history of philosophy.

The relation of philosophy and religion is, historically speaking, a dialectical relation which shows philosophy and religion in constant conflict. While Greek philosophy had signified a silent triumph over the Homeric tradition of religion and the Greek religion as a whole, the establishment of Christianity later was a loud triumph of religion over philosophy. The first triumph was the triumph of free reason, and the second one the triumph of an enforced faith.

The closure of the Neo-platonic school by the Christian emperor Justinian in 529 was probably the most obvious example of this enforced faith. The philosophers of the eliminated school fled to Persia and started to teach at the University of Gondi Shapour, where Christian swords could not follow them any longer.

The conflict went on. Good Christian thinkers however, who wanted to be at the same time Christians and philosophers, played a reconciliatory role to bring the two contradictory parties together. Thomas Aquinas was one of them. He incorporated Reason and Revelation into a unity, a unity, however, which was covering a pronounced duality. Reason was applied and acknowledged but not as a master of reality but as a slave of Revelation. The "Revelation of Truth" could not be challenged by anyone or anything, not even by Reason.

Philosophy had a new struggle for emancipation. The emancipation however did not come sooner than the 17th century and was not completely realized until the middle of the 19th century and the breakdown of Idealism.

The emancipation of philosophy from theology won its relative victory by the rational foundation of Descartes' philosophy, and still more by Spinoza's daring efforts to draw a distinctive line between religion and philosophy.

A careful study of the Scripture led Spinoza to believe that those articles of faith demonstrated as miracles and mythological stories, were not to be held logically. The daring man confesses that he was still not daring enough to say everything:

> "If I were to enumerate all the passages of Scripture addressed only to individuals, or to a particular man's understanding, and which cannot, without great danger to philosophy, be defended as divine doctrines, I should go far beyond the brevity at which I aim."[1]

------

[1] Spinoza, Benedict. *Theological—Political Treatise.* R. H. M. Elwes, Translator. New York, 1951, p. 42.

Spinoza's main polemic is directed against those thinkers who had applied philosophy to defend the Scripture. Philosophy as a matter of reason, he thought, was not supposed to come to the aid of religion which was a matter of faith. And this, as he claimed, was the chief aim of his Theological Treatise.[2] To defend the Scripture by reason would mean, said Spinoza, "to invoke the aid of reason for her own defeat."[3]

If philosophy as a matter of reason is the instrument of rational conviction, religion, which is an instrument of obedience, can never be considered as philosophy. To that effect Spinoza wrote:

"I will remark that Moses did not seek to convince the Jews by reason, but bound them by a covenant, by oath, and by conferring benefits; further, he threatened the people with punishment if they should infringe the law, and promised rewards if they should obey it. All these are not means for teaching knowledge, but for inspiring obedience."[4]

As a consequence of this and other observations Spinoza confirms his basic thesis:

"It remains for me to show that between faith or theology, and philosophy, there is no connection, or affinity. I think no one will dispute the fact, who has knowledge of the aim and foundations of the two subjects, for they are as wide apart as the poles."[5]

And he explores this point further:

"The sphere of reason is, as we have said truth and wisdom; the sphere of theology is piety and obedience."[6]

---

[2] *Ibid.*, p. 183.
[3] *Ibid.*, p. 197.
[4] *Ibid.*, p. 183.
[5] *Ibid.*, p. 189.
[6] *Ibid.*, p. 194.

Reason Replaces Faith

This separation of philosophy and theology was the first decisive introduction to the emancipation of philosophy from theology. In other words, emancipation was the logical consequence of separation. The logic of this emancipation was the logic of history.

The assumption that history is a progressive development, would justify the emancipation of philosophy as a development in progress. The history of the intellectual progress of the human mind, is the history of realization of his independence; philosophy as the intellectual negation to his religious submission is the consciousness of his independence. It is the foundation of his freedom, the knowledge of his reality, and in true sense his self-consciousness.

The idealist philosophy of the 19th Century explored this self-consciousness of mankind as a consciousness of God. The dominative Pantheistic elements of this philosophy had identified the reality of man with the reality of God in a mystical fashion. This identification was practically a departure from the monistic understanding of God in favor of the Pantheistic approach of Spinoza. And this was a step beyond religion.

Spinoza who had criticized Moses for having searched God on the top of a mountain disregarding the fact that God was "omnipresent,"[7] was now influencing the mind of Hegel to demonstrate a march of God in history.[8]

This march, which in a sense demonstrated a humanization of God, was to produce nothing less than a Godly human. This again was a step beyond religion. Hegel placed

---

[7] *Ibid.*, p. 38.
[8] Hegel. *Philosophy of History, Introduction.*

philosophy beyond religion as he classified the developing stages of the absolute mind, to indicate the dialectical superiority of philosophy to religion.

The beginning of the 19th Century was, therefore, the period of reversing the order of religion and philosophy. This order was no longer religion-philosophy, but philosophy-religion. The emancipated philosophy now had started to dominate religion.

Restoration of Human Reality

I. *Marxism*

Modern Idealism parted from religion by eliminating the gulf which had previously existed between man and God as his absolute reality. The breakdown of Idealism later, was the breakdown of this absolute reality; a further development of philosophy thus indicated a further emancipation of mankind. Natural science, which had also been relieved from the captivity of theology, was now assisting philosophy to establish its demand. A philosophical-scientific revolt against religion appeared to become a revolt against God.

Marxism by advocating dialectical materialism was one representation of this revolt. Its challenge to German idealism was from the beginning a challenge of religion, which according to Marx had generated the idealistic mind of Hegel.

The ambition of Marx was the establishment of a religion of man as opposed to that of God. And this was the phenomenological basis of his historical materialism.

In his Critique of Hegel's Philosophy of Right, he considers the criticism of religion "the premise of all criticism."[9]

---

[9] Marx, Karl. *Early Writings.* T. B. Bottomre, Translator. New York: McGraw Hill Book Company, 1964, p. 43.

And under the influence of Feuerbach, he explores the notion of the man-made religion:

> "Man, who has found in the fantastic reality of heavens, where he sought in supernatural being, only his own reflection, will no longer be tempted to find only the semblance of himself—a non human being—where he seeks and must seek his true reality."[10]

While, according to Idealism, the real being of man was to be found in the reality of God, according to Marxism God was, as non-human, a denial of the reality of man. It was the self-alienation of man.

> "Religion is indeed man's self-consciousness and self-awareness so long as he has not found himself or has lost himself again."[11]

The concept of God is accordingly the concept of a lost identity, a notion of alienation which is nothing more than a negation of man. Man, in order to find himself, has to lose God. The elimination of God would therefore mean a restoration of man.

Dialectical materialism was so far a success in establishing bases for the restoration of man to his true reality. But, as we will see, this restoration of man from God was used only as a steppingstone for his further alienation.

In other words, rejecting the interpretation of man in terms of "God," "religion" and "idea," was to establish a premise for the interpretation of man in terms of "matter," "economics" and "materialistic determinism." It was a matter of restoring man from one alien to another one, from God to matter! Was "matter" really the reality of man?

II. *Philosophy of Nietzsche*

Another basic position of modern philosophy against reli-

---

[10] *Ibid.*
[11] *Ibid.*

gion is the position taken by Friedrich Nietzsche. Nietzsche
with his daring demand: a Revaluation of all Values,[12] may
be regarded as the most serious philosophical challenge
against religion. He was more ambitious and at the same
time more optimistic than Marx about human being. While
Marx believed in restoration mankind to his "true" reality by
eliminating the concept of God from his consciousness,
Nietzsche considered this elimination as a condition to enable
man to overcome his reality.

Man's reality according to Nietzsche had been a reality of
decay and degeneration. Christianity with its "immoral morality" which Nietzsche describes as slave morality, has enslaved
human nature. An emancipation from such an enslavement
should, at the same time, mean an emancipation from his
reality. Man was to overcome his master and his own slave
reality at the same time.

As a man of future, he had to overcome himself and to
become superman. And for that matter God had to die first.
As long as a God lives, mankind is weak, feminine and cor-
rupted by morality of humility and forgiveness. The living
God therefore must leave, or man is not worthy of living.

The following is Nietzsche's famous passage of his Zarathustra concerning the death of God.[13]

"Before God!—Now however this God hath died! Ye higher
men, this God was your greatest danger.

Only since he lay in the grave have Ye again arisen. Now
only cometh the great noontide, now, only doth the higher man
become master!

Well! Take heart! Ye higher men! First now travaileth the
mountain of the human future. God hath died: Now do *we*
desire the Superman to live.

---

[12] Nietzsche, Friedrich. The Subtitle of His Major Work: "Der Wille
Zur Macht."

[13] Nietzsche, Friedrich, *Also Sprach Zarathustra.* Kroner Verlag Stutt-
gart, 1956, p. 318. English Translation.

The most careful ask today: 'How is man to be maintained?'
Zarathustra however asketh, as the first and only one: 'How
is man to be surpassed?'

The Superman, I have at heart, that is the first and only thing
to me—and not man: not the neighbour, not the poorest, not
the sorriest, not the best."

God and especially Christian God is interpreted as the
source of human weakness. Nietzsche's philosophy is demanding a revaluation of all values based upon and derived from
Christian doctrines. Life was to emancipate itself from all
these and similar principles and from all systems of philosophy
which tried to hold on to those principles. Life as a changing
process could not have any everlasting principle except that
of change. And Nietzsche's New Concept of Universe provides a natural scientific basis for this principle change. On
the scientific ground of the "everlastingness of energy," he
rejects the notion of a beginning and an end in relation to
the universe. This way he develops a concept of eternity out
of the concept of time. Time becomes eternity and this is
the eternity that Nietzsche loves: It is the foundation of the
"Permanent Recurrence." Let him speak for himself:

"The universe exists, it is nothing that grows into existence and
passes out of existence, or, better still, it develops, it passes
away, but it never began to develop, and has never ceased from
passing away, it maintains itself in both states . . . It lives on
itself, its excrements are its nourishment.
We need not concern ourselves for one instant with the hypothesis of a *created world*. The concept "create" is today utterly
indefinable and unrealizable; it is but a word which hails from
superstitious ages; nothing can be explained with a word . . .
to speak metaphysically, if becoming could resolve itself into
being or into non-entity, this state ought already to have been
reached. But it has not been reached, it therefore follows . . ."[14]

---

[14] Nietzsche, Friedrich. *Wille Zur Macht*. Kroner Verlag Leipzig, 1930.
Selection from English Translation.

Such a concept of universe is one of the concepts of the modern philosophy which excludes religion or any philosophy following the footprint of religion.

Philosophy as Religion

Modern philosophy as a negation of the old religion is establishing itself as a new religion. The God of the new religion is human being, who with or without a hidden faith in a hidden God is searching for "himself." His possible relation to a possible God is not of reliance. Its only reliance tends to be self-reliance. This is what he had been trying to establish. And for this reason he had been constantly challenged.

Every challenge aimed at his self-alienation and by dominating him, made him something that he was not, something other than himself! Every challenge was a challenge of alienation which robbed his consciousness and provided him with a false consciousness. Consequently he in every period of self-alienation thought of himself to be something that he was not, and did not think of himself as something that he was.

His first challenge was nature and his primitive mind had to accept nature's terms and consider his own reality accordingly. This was his first self-alienation and his highest degree of weakness.

Then God a supernatural power restored his consciousness but not to him as man but to himself as God. Man's consciousness of himself was only a subordinate consciousness of God. He was not really he.

Then "matter," in the shape of economic foundation of man's society tried to make his nature known to himself by relieving him from the unknown God of religion. It tried to define for him his self-consciousness. But how could an "it" explain *"his"* self-consciousness? If "he" is defined by "it," then he is still not himself. This way the restored human is alienated again. Materialism which saved him once, cannot save him again. Nor can it give him any explanation why it cannot.

The explanation has to come from a different philosophical observation, from a philosophy which considers all differences of alienation and does not side with any. The philosophy which indicates the possibility of a constant negation of human nature and the necessity of a constant "turning back to himself." The philosophy of constant alienation and constant restoration. In one way it is religion. It is a faith but the faith of man in himself and in his Individuality.

A true religion must be a religion which considers "man" as reality, a changing reality which changes with reality. A reality which goes through changes and yet remains real. He is accordingly a constant growth and regrowth. With him grow also his problems and with his problems the solutions to his problems. These problems and solutions are not reducible to one or two or many. They are endless. Their endlessness is a consequence of the endlessness of life. The secular life!

Such a secular life can only be explained and explored by a secular religion. It *needs* therefore a secular religion. It needs philosophy.

V

Freedom in Art:
A Prospective in Aesthetics

LAST SUMMER at a philosophical seminar of the Free University of Berlin, the very old question of philosophy: Free Will and Determinism, was put to discussion. The exchange of the philosophical arguments could hardly add anything new to the already existing thoughts concerning this everlasting problem in the history of philosophy.

Among the energetic debaters, I met a young German artist who, without having any particular background in philosophy, could bring the seminar to a suggestive approach. His suggested solution to the problem was artistic, while his intended conclusion was philosophical. He made this general question of philosophy a question of Aesthetics and gave, with no reservations, a positive answer to it: mankind is free. In order to reach this conclusion he tried to establish an identical relationship between the concepts of creativeness and freedom. He maintained that the human mind was free as long as it was creative and as often as it created.

To him, an artist was the best example of a creative mind and art the most convincing proof for human freedom.

While religion had made the general life of man subject to predestination, and science left him hanging between free will and determinism, art as a supplement of nature gave him the opportunity of supplementing natural freedom. "When I paint," he said, "I have my freest moments. I am most free when I am most creative. Even nature cannot take this freedom away. I do not have to follow nature even when I present nature. In this presentation I am able to paint the colors that I think an object should have and not the color it has in reality."

This concept of artistic freedom, while presented to provide an answer to a general question of philosophy, was itself subject to a general question: Is an artist as an artist really free? And this question leads us to a variety of questions: What is the concept of art as related to that of freedom? Is art a free expression of a free mind or is it subject to a determinism of some kind: historical scientific or logical? Is art a manifestation of the deterministic spirit of time? Is it a changeable dictate of a historical necessity, or is it a timeless absolute product of a creative mind? And this last question takes us back to our first. Is the creative mind itself free? This way, and finally, the question of a free art itself becomes a question of philosophy. In other words the solution to a problem of philosophy develops into a problem of art which itself needs a philosophical solution.

The Answer of Philosophy to the Question of Artistic Freedom

A search into the history of philosophy provides us with almost as many different opinions on the subject as there are different philosophies. Despite the numerous variations, however, the basic philosophical reflections on this question may be classified into two main categories: 1. the deterministic tendencies 2. theories of artistic freedom.

The deterministic tendencies are themselves subject to a basic division by regarding: a) art as a discipline of philosophical-logical regulations, and b) art as a subject of historical or economic determinism.

a) *Art as a discipline of philosophical-logical regulations.* The best illustration for this view is the famous case of ancient time: Plato vs. Homer, as an early example of philosophical tyranny against art.

Plato in his philosophy of the state determined what a poet must do and what he must not do. "He must say that God did what was just and right."[1] And in order to make sure of that, Plato suggested: "The first thing will be to establish a censorship of the works of fiction, and let the censors receive any tale of fiction which is good, and reject the bad."[2] And further: "The founder of a state ought to know the general form in which poets should cast their tales, and the limits which *must* be observed by them . . ."[3]

Homer, a poet who had not obeyed this philosophical "must," was therefore condemned. This condemnation was based upon a dualistic philosophical principle according to which Plato recognized God as the author of only good things. Homer's description of Zeus as "the dispenser of good and evil"[4] was a negation of Plato's dualistic principle. His poetry had not expressed what Plato believed to be a philosophical "truth."

The so-called philosophical "truth" motivated the Greek philosopher to pass laws indicating how the poets had to think. "Let this then be one of our rules and principles concerning the gods, to which our poets and reciters will be ex-

---

1 Plato. *Dialogues.* B. Jowett, Translator. New York, 1942, p. 283.
2 *Ibid.,* p. 279.
3 *Ibid.*
4 *Ibid.,* p. 282.

pected to conform. That God is not the author of all things, but of good only." Contrary to the regular laws which only apply to the present and future cases, the self-made laws of Plato applied also to the past and condemned Homer in his grave!

b) *Art as subject of economic and historical determinism.* The philosophical tyrannization of art was not only limited to the Plato of the ancient time, it extended also to the world views of modern Platos such as Marx and Lenin.

Briefly speaking, human mind according to Marxism is determined by factors "indispensable and independent of his will."[5] These factors are material powers of production as derived from the economic structure of a society. The real foundation of a human life is this social-economic structure to which culture is only a secondary phenomenon.

When Marx argues that "the mode of production on material life determines the general character of the social-political and spiritual processes of life," he certainly includes art in this general subjection to economic and historical determinism. Marx is specific in pointing out that: "It is not the consciousness of men that determines their existence, but, on the contrary, their social existence determines their consciousness."[6]

As a particular expression of human consciousness, art is also determined by the social structure of human existence. By looking at the economic foundation of a society, we should be able to comprehend its cultural life and artistic production. The dialectical description of the necessary changes of economic history is, at the same time, an explanation for artistic developments in history. The artist has, therefore, no choice except to follow a fixed pattern of historical necessities and timely requirements. He, even in his artistic activ-

---

[5] Karl Marx. *Critique of Political Economy,* preface. N. E. Stone, Translator. P. 11.
[6] *Ibid.*

ities, is not to lead, but to be led. And what leads him is not a superior intelligence, not a more powerful creative mind, but a mere economic machinery. He may *will* only what is already determined; he can do only what he is forced to do. He is again a slave. This time, however, his master is not the philosophical brain of a Plato, but the brainless machine of an economic foundation. The philosopher, this time, did not enslave him directly; he assigned him a master, who is at the same time his own master. Marxism as a philosophy is a rationalized subjection to a master called *necessity*. It is a self-enslavement in favor of fate. And philosophy forced art into this fatal destiny of its own. It challenged artistic freedom. It imposed its self-imposed *"must"* also upon art. Lenin, very much in Plato's fashion, described this "must."

> "Literature *must* become Party literature . . . Down with non-partisan literatures! Down with superman literature! Literature must become a part of the general cause of the proletariat, 'a small cog and a small screw' in the social democratic mechanism, one and indivisible—a mechanism set in motion by the entire conscious vanguard of the whole working class. Literature must become an integral part of the organized, methodical, and unified labors of the Social Democratic Party."[7]

Literature, according to Lenin's philosophy, had to become a party literature, since philosophy had become a party philosophy. Philosophy's highest task in its highest stage of perfection, according to Marxism-Leninism, was to elaborate and to justify the world outlook of the proletariat's revolution. Marxism, therefore, was regarded as the only valid philosophy and Marx as the only true philosopher. Every other philosophy was regarded as a philosophy of the dominating classes which, by the elimination of the classes and by the establishment of a classless society, would automatically disappear.

This exclusion of philosophies from philosophy, this self-

[7] Aezel and Meray. Statement of Lenin, Novaia jizm in *The Revolt of the Mind*. New York, 1959, p. vi.

evaluation of Marxism, is practically a reduction of philosophy to ideology. And only a reduction of philosophy to ideology would result in a philosophical tyrannization of art. In order to confine itself to this particularized philosophy, the world vision of the artist would lose its essential generality. Philosophy as ideology determines what the artist *should do* and how the artistic mind *should express* itself. The condemnation of non-ideological philosophy applies also to non-ideological art. Art, like every other human production, had its origin, its concept, its purpose, its form, its technique, and also its technical justification in one ideology and one ideology alone. The artist had to follow the rules expressed by a party leadership.

The deterministic explanation of artistic production is not limited only to Marxism and economic determinism; it is a general application of historical determinism. Whatever the indicating factor of this so-called historical deterministic progress, whether it is materialistic foundation of society or God's mind, it is the determination of *time*. The artistic creation is accordingly regulated strongly by the factor of time and its main characteristics. This theory leaves hardly any room for a concept of the free function of the artistic mind.

2. Theories of artistic freedom. The most influential theories of freedom in art are developed by Immanuel Kant in his "Critique of the Aesthetical Judgment." The basic hypothesis of this work is derived from the theory of judgment. After defining taste as the faculty of judging the beautiful,[8] Kant describes how different this judgment is from a logical understanding. An aesthetical judgment is as far removed from a logical understanding as Aesthetics is from Logic. In his own words: "The judgment of taste is . . . not a judgment of cognition, and is consequently not logical but aesthetical by

---

[8] Immanuel Kant. *The Critique of Judgment.* J. C. Meredith, Translator. Oxford, 1952, p. 50.

which we understand that whose determining ground can be no other than subjective."[9]

That a judgment of taste is subjective means simply that it is singular. It is the function of the individual judging mind which, in making its judgment, applies no general principle and consequently no "concept."

The application of any general concept or any concept in general, would, according to Kant, change the aesthetical judgment to a logical judgment. An expression such as "roses, in general, are beautiful" is no more simply aesthetical, but primarily logical.[10] The pure aesthetical judgment would refer to an individual beauty alone: "this rose is beautiful." The conflicting characters of "logical" and "aesthetical" are here presented as general and particular. It is only the case of generality which provides us with concepts, and aesthetical judgments do not follow concepts.

"If we judge objects merely according to concepts, then all representation of beauty is lost."[11] This individual understanding of beauty as judgment leads us to the notion of individual presentation of beauty as creation. It brings us to the creative subject; to the artistic mind!

The essential particularly of an art-product is the particular representation of the individual mind of the artist. Nothing except this distinguished individuality of the artistic mind can express its originality. The originality of the artist is therefore explored through his individuality as a genius. Kant's own description of genius makes this point clearer: ". . . Genius is a talent for producing that for which no definite rule can be given, it is not a mere aptitude for what can be learned by a rule. Hence originality must be its first property."[12] Another passage states: "Genius is the exemplary

---

[9] *Ibid.*, p. 42.
[10] *Ibid.*, p. 55.
[11] *Ibid.*, p. 56.

originality of the natural gifts of a subject in the *free employ-
ment of his cognitive faculties.*"[13]

The originality of genius remains beyond all rules and
regulations. It is the originality itself which gives rule to art,
and in giving this rule it is free of all rules. Without this
philosophical element of freedom, the concept of originality
is a mere self-contradiction.

Kant's notion of originality as a justification of artistic
freedom is a philosophical denunciation of what he called
"arbitrary rules."[14] Art as a free product is similar to nature.
"In a product of beautiful art, we must become conscious
that it is art and not nature; but yet the purposiveness in its
forms must seem to be as free from all constraints of arbitrary rules as if it were a product of nature."[15]

Synthesis of Determinism and Freedom

Kant's theory of artistic freedom, despite its suggestive
nature and sound foundation, does not solve the existing
problem entirely. His identification of art and nature, no
matter how broad his concept of nature may be, implies a
limitation of the concept of art. It provides us, moreover,
only with the natural foundation of art and overlooks its
social and historical origins. Kant's failure to recognize the
social foundation of art would lead to a total separation of
art from ideology. The artist would become, therefore, a creative mind without a purpose, a genius without a concept,

---

12 *Ibid.*, p. 186.
13 *Ibid.*, p. 181.
14 *Ibid.*, p. 166.
15 *Ibid.*, p. 167

and a world-personality without a world-vision. While Lenin imposes one particular ideology on the artist's mind, Kant deprives him from practically all ideologies. Kant and Lenin are the presentation of two extreme and contradictory cases.

With reference to Kant's overlooking the social foundation of art, we need further consideration. If the individual artist is of any relation to his social environment, then he is not only "the exemplary originality of the natural gifts." He belongs as much to nature as to society and as much to society as to time. His mind and his aesthetic ideas are subjects of the timely elements of *becoming*. He was not *born* as an artist, but with artistic talent; his becoming an artist was the application of his life history. It was the work of time. Even his timeless works are stamped by time, even his great historical personality is a product of history. The paintings of the Renaissance period demonstrate a particular characteristic; the characteristic of a particular time as different from and opposed to the previous tradition. So was it also the case of the Romantic poetry, for example, expressing the spirit of the Romantic Age. We read a poem and we know to which period it belongs, we see a painting and we realize what timely characteristic it represents. The artist, therefore, in expressing himself expresses also his time and his timely inspirations. And that is what Kant's philosophy did not explain.

On the other hand the case of determinism is also a one-sided case of inadequate explanation. It shows logical defectiveness by failing to establish a firm position.

If art as an expressed consciousness of human mind is a mere determination of time (be it economic, social or otherwise), what makes this expression subject to essential variation at one time? What establishes a substantial identity between one particular artist and his work? Why are the individual particularities of one artistic mind so pronouncedly different from those of the other?

We see the stamp of the time upon all important artistic works, but we also see the name of the individual artist next to it. This does not indicate a mere name, it is the identity of a creative soul. Expert eyes could recognize any possible undiscovered painting of Rembrandt and identify it both with Rembrandt's person and Rembrandt's time.

The identity of an art product is, therefore, a matter of both *timely particularity* and *artistic personality*. It is this basic notion of *duality* which constitutes and demonstrates artistic originality.

The philosophers of aesthetic freedom forget that when the artist creates he creates in time. The deterministic thinker, on the other hand, does not realize that without an artistic mind there may not be any art product. While, however, in neither of the two cases do we find a complete truth, in both cases we find some distinguished moments of truth. Truth is a combination of both or none. Truth is their synthesis.

The history of art in general can provide us with numerous examples of this synthetic analysis. Among all these, however, I would refer only to two.

The music of Chopin often described as "music of freedom" was, to a great extent, a revolutionary expression of Poland's national spirit. Against the Russian domination of the country, the popular Polish resistance manifested itself as the revolution of 1830. Russian reinforcement and the fall of Warsaw one year later motivated the artist in composing his famous work. His Etude in C Minor (Opus 10, No. 12), is generally supposed to be inspired by the 1831 event. With this reference one of the Chopin biographers wrote:

> "His music was even more national than the words of his countrymen, and has remained the avenue through which the love and sympathy of the outside world have poured for the best part of a century of Poland's misery. No wonder that Polish people honour Chopin as their greatest son."[16]

---

[16] Murdoch, William. *Chopin: His Life*. New York, 1953, p. 108.

Chopin was not only a son of his nation but also the son of his time. The society of his time determined the nature of his inspiration but the nature of his inspiration alone. The rest was the determination of his own creative mind. Chopin would not have produced an Etude in C Minor if there had not been a fall of Warsaw in 1831. Nor could the fall of Warsaw have inspired an Etude in C Minor if there was not a creative mind called Chopin.

The question again is a question of double particularity: particularity of mind and particularity of time. And these two together describe the artistic originality of a Polish musician.

My second example refers to another revolutionary musician demonstrating a reconciliatory relation between the timely indication and artistic freedom. Here, too, the indication of time and the objective of the music which it inspired was freedom. This is the example of the Hungarian musician of the 19th century Erkel and his famous opera: Heroic People.

Under the revolutionary conditions of Europe and shortly before the universal revolution of 1848 this opera was composed. The revolution with its anti-monarchial and anti-feudalistic aims, following the examples of France, Germany and Austria broke out also in Hungary. It is interesting to notice that the revolution started directly from the Budapest opera house where the opera "Heroic People" was being performed. The following events, such as the execution of the King (Franz Albrecht, the brother of the Austrian King ruling in his name in Hungary), were a realization of the story of the opera. The 1956 Hungarian revolution also witnessed a further influence of Erkel's opera in actual situation of the country. Hungarian people destroyed the statue of Stalin while singing the revolutionary parts of that opera.

Here again the factor of time and the will of the artist had formed a double originality as a synthetic freedom. The "Heroic People" opera was the original product of the situation of 1848 and the artist Erkel. With the situation of 1848 or with Erkel alone the opera of "Heroic People" would not have been composed. Maybe a different opera or a similar opera but never the same opera.

"THE OPPRESSOR IS DEAD"
from Heroic People by Ferenc Erkel

The infidel king is slain,
The dark era is done.
Our country can breathe now,
For liberty and the people are reunited.

Listen, Hungarians!

This is the dawning of the bright new morn,
A beautiful beginning, a newborn sun
Which can never wane,
For the oppressor is dead.

Listen, wide world!

The oppressor is dead.
A ray of new hope brightens our day.
The people and liberty are joined once more.
Let it remain so for eternity.

The Exceptional Case of the Exceptional Geniuses

The theory of aesthetic synthesis is generally but not necessarily always true. There are instances that the synthetic balance of freedom and determinism is disturbed and one of the two dominates the other. The artistic mind would be in its highest stage of self mastery and creation, should the element of freedom prevail. Genius establishes then his own aesthetic determination against time. In this case, however, it is not so much freedom as it is power which the genius exercises. The question of freedom consequently, becomes a question of self-mastery of art. And it is this undisputable self-mastery which establishes an exceptional artistic freedom. The artistic mind liberates itself from the tyranny of the time by first conquering it. This idea of an established freedom as self-mastery, is different from the general theories of freedom which describe the aesthetic movement as a consequence of freedom. According to the new idea, *freedom itself* is the consequence of the aesthetic movement. The artistic mind in order to be completely free, conquers the time and this conquering of time is itself an aesthetic movement. It obtains freedom. The degree of this obtained freedom depends on the strength of the conquest. And this whole idea is derived from the definition of life as "will to power."

The definition of Life as "will to power" was a new introduction to the philosophy of 19th century by Friedrich Nietzsche. While the application of Nietzsche's time was still that of a stubbornly surviving romanticism, and the newly developed dialectical materialism, his philosophy selected an independent direction of both. The psychological principle of "will to power" was a counter to "dialectical necessity" as well as Darwin's theory of evolution. It signified an aesthetic revolt against any logical or biological domination, it suggested a "revaluation of all values" and a re-formation of all Forms!

One of the central principles of Nietzsche's philosophy of life was aesthetics. As a poet-philosopher he considered art as a means of elevation of life in establishing superior values. The ideas of "higher man" as the legislature of future and the rosy future of human life, for example, are philosophic and artistic reflections of a powerful mind, which is elevated beyond the present time. Not a Richard Wagner who, according to Nietzsche, surrendered himself to the feminine sentimentality of the time, but a strong masculine artistic mind who would take revenge of Wagner's "weak music" was the artist of that rosy future.[17] He would dominate the timely domination of romanticism, he would degenerate the existing degeneration, he would conquer Wagner. Conquering Wagner meant conquering the time which conquered Wagner and made him, in Nietzsche's words, "kneel before the Christian cross."[18]

Such a condemnation of the condemning life, such an aesthetic nihilism was a constructive positive step towards a superior life. This close association between the two concepts: life and art, would develop a philosophy of art out of the philosophy of life. As a consequence of an identical relation between these two, the principle definition of life as will to power applies also to art. Artistic production became therefore power production. The conquering artist, like Nietzsche himself, intends to conquer the time through his aesthetic power. Here the exclusive destiny of art is to conquer the time or to be conquered by it. In this case artistic production is no longer the partner of time, it is rather its rival, its enemy.

The self-mastered artist does not accept a partnership with time when time is a representation of social corruption. Under a topic such as "The Return Home" he advocates a return to himself, he means to depart from all corruptive productions of time. Only through successful struggle with the time can he express his originality, and establish his self mastery. And only when he establishes his superior aesthetic values is he free.

How often does this dominating freedom as free domination come to expression? As often as he can express his undisputed aesthetic vigor. And Nietzsche's own writings provide us with many examples. I quote only one.

"Here fly open unto me all being's words and word-cabinets: Here all being wanteth to become words, here all becoming wanteth to learn of me how to talk."[19]

While writing in the depth of his imaginative silence, his silent imagination explained his individual self mastery as a deeply creative lonesomeness. Here the poet-philosopher showed "all being" how to become his words and "all becoming" how to submit to his expression. He was free.

---

[17] Nietzsche, Friedrich. *Menschliches Allzumenschliches.* Kroner Verlag, Leipzig, 1930, Second Part, p. 7.

[18] *Ibid.,* p. 6.

[19] Nietzsche, Friedrich. *Thus Spake Zarathustra.* Thomas Common, Translator. New York: The Modern Library, p. 204.

VI

Life as Creativeness

ACCORDING TO THE 19th Century philosopher Schelling, human history is a drama with God as its chief author and men as co-authors and actors.[1] The whole act of creation is a work of art which manifests the artistic mind of its Creator. Schelling's method of Transcendental Idealism is to explore the movement of transcending quality of creativeness which elevates the artistic mind of man to the artistic mind of God. Man is a creature who creates and thus assimilates the Creator on basis of identical power of creativeness.

Schelling's Transcendental Idealism which develops ultimately into a "Philosophy of Identity," presents, as its main objective, a solution to the problem of "contrasts." It starts from the viewpoint of a pre-established harmony between the contradictory orders of "real and ideal," "subject and object" and "mind and nature"[2] and it finally reaches the point of a re-established harmony between all contrasts.

The re-establishment of this harmony is the function of the drama of history. The drama is artistic and philosophical.

---

[1] Hofstadter, Albert. *Philosophies of Art and Beauty*. New York: The Modern Library, 1964, p. 346.

[2] *Ibid.*, p. 359.

It is philosophical in concept and artistic in function. It represents the concept of reunity and the function of re-creation. It re-creates the previously created and later distorted harmony of things and thoughts.

The case of history is a case of artistic philosophical co-operation. In the course of this dramatic development the task of philosophy is to internalize "nature" and the action of art is to externalize "mind." Thus philosophy would become a discipline of subjective reflection and art a method of objective presentation.[3] In Schelling's own words:

> "If art is deprived of objectivity, one may say it ceases to be what it is and becomes philosophy; give objectivity to philosophy, it ceases to be philosophy and becomes art."[4]

This interchangeability of art and philosophy is an expression of their essential affinity which makes it possible to incorporate them into a unitary system: the system of Transcendental Idealism. And this is the act of the drama of history which, as already mentioned, is to re-establish a pre-established unity. It ends where it starts. And Schelling proudly considers this circular movement as a justification of his system.

> "A system is completed when it has returned to its starting point."[5]

And this is a characteristic of his own system.

A careful examination of Schelling's idealist philosophy of art should lead us to the following consequences:

1. Art is a method of re-creation.
2. Art follows a metaphysical aim and therefore a destiny.
3. In following this destiny it is bound to follow a philosophical system called Transcendental Idealism.

---

[3] *Ibid.*, p. 356.
[4] *Ibid.*, p. 375.
[5] *Ibid.*, p. 374.

Yet the artistic mind of man is called by Schelling the "co-author" of the drama of history! And in addition to that, man is supposedly exercising a free function of creativity!

A critical observation of Schelling's system however, shows how seriously the freedom of the artistic mind is challenged by the implications of this system.

To begin with, the most serious threat to artistic freedom is the "system" itself, that of Schelling or those of others. An artificial attempt, a forced intention to complete a system may be called a forced philosophy of some kind but not art. A system in order to be a system must be closed or, as Schelling says, complete. But art is neither complete nor closed. Art represents something open and something continuous, something developing and something changing. Art represents "life" and that is precisely why it cannot represent "the system." If art is forced to represent a closed system, it is then the art of a closed system and not the art of life.

By the growth of philosophies of life, philosophical systems are gradually losing their applicability. "Escaping systems" is an artistic philosophical movement of this growth. It has traditions, continuity and future. Already in the course of philosophical developments of the 19th Century, Soren Kierkegaard and Friedrich Nietzsche succeeded in establishing foundations for a philosophy of life as opposed to philosophies of "systems." This movement was to emancipate art and philosophy from all impositions of all "systems" upon life. All "final purposes," all "divine destinies," all "a priori principles" which have previously denoted "life" into lifeless "abstractions," were to be rejected.

The modern philosophical movement of emancipation is the heart of the modern history and as such, itself a part of the "Human Drama" which Schelling refers to. Now, would Schelling's philosophy of "identity" consider this historical

challenge also as a problem of "contrast" which itself finds
its ultimate solution within the drama? or should the philosophy of "identity" dismiss the challenge for falling totally
out of the scope of the closed "system"?

With reference to both of these alternatives one can ask
a further question: how can a system include solutions in its
jurisdiction which are excluded from its domain as problems?
How can a negation of Transcendental Idealism be ever identified? or, on the other hand, how can a challenge of negation which is historically established be ignored?

The challenge remains. Yet my purpose in choosing
Schelling is not only to present him with a challenge. I also
want to explore the interpretive contributions which his philosophy of art would make to the idea of creativeness, should
this philosophy lose its metaphysical impositions. Then a
single hypothesis such as: "art as re-creation" would be enough
to make him a modern philosopher of art.

Also, one can follow the impressive doctrine of Schelling's
"drama" should the "drama" stop following his system. Thus
I would consider the artistic man as existing being the true
author of this "drama," then I would call this drama a drama
of freedom.

According to Wilhelm Dilthey art is an expression of
life.[6] Accepting this non-metaphysical conception and considering "creativity" as the main characteristic of life, we may
easily establish our main subject of inquiry: *life as creativeness.*

The process of life is a process of endless continuity. It
is a "drama" indeed, but a drama with no beginning and no
end. It is the timely drama of infinity. We are moving from
an endless past to an endless future.

The present is nothing but our presence, and the present

---

6 Dilthey, Wilhelm. *Pattern and Meaning in History* (H. P. Rickman,
editor). New York: Harper Torchbooks, 1962, p. 68.

is eternity. One may say with Dilthey: "Only in the present is there fullness of time and therefore fullness of life."[7] And there is a future constantly filling the present and materializing its fullness on a permanent basis. Or as the historian Ferguson believes:

"The fleeting present is ever the transitional link through which all our yesterdays flow uninterruptedly into the infinite succession of tomorrow and tomorrow and tomorrow."[8]

Life is the infinity of this continuous succession. The continuity of succession is a continuity of events caused by "will" or by chance, or by "will in rejection or acceptance of chance." It is only in the dynamic functions of will that creativity originates. And it is mainly the purposive nature of man which initiates his actions. Culture and its growing patterns are colorful manifestations of this living and creating will, especially art which is the blossom of man's culture. Art is "will" in its freest and most productive expression.

The individual artist is a creature of culture who creates. Among all those who live, the artist is the freest; hence he is the liveliest. The degree of his liveliness is precisely the degree of his creativity. He is the most vigorous actor and the most original author of human "drama." He is the acting author whose action is as strong as his imagination. His aesthetic vigor is his freedom and his freedom his life: the life of free creativity. Take his freedom away, and you have taken his creativity and with it his life. But what is a creative life? To answer this question one has to analyze the concept of the aesthetic movement:

The aesthetic movement of creativity consists of three distinct yet harmonious functions: "overcoming," "re-production" and "elevation." It is through the continuity of these

---

[7] *Ibid.*, p. 99.

[8] Ferguson, Wallace K. *Renaissance, Toward the Modern State.* New York: Harper and Row, 1962, p. 3.

combined functions that art establishes its substantial relationship with life. It reflects life and it reflects on life. It follows life and it leads life. It speaks to life and speaks as life. It is life in its most elaborated expression of self-reflection. Let us now examine all three functions with reference to life.

A. *Art as overcoming*

It is in its particular sense of phenomenological negation that the conception of "art as creativeness" leads to the notion of "art as overcoming." Art in its general sense of creativity has no other aim than to establish its own reality in contra-distinction to all forms of reality. True art does not imitate nature. True art is the follower of its own truth. It re-produces nature and in order to do so it has first to overcome nature. It is the creative lightning whose primary function is destruction: in that it destroys it creates. It might shine a moment but that is a shining moment of infinity: a moment of destructive creativeness. The artist is the constructive destroyer whose value is to negate all negative values. He negates negation, he destroys destruction. He pours joy into suffering and derives the beauty of life out of the life of beauty. Even by expressing sorrow, he overcomes sorrow, even by re-creating suffering he dominates suffering. He is the vigorous artist of optimism whose expressions are the expression of will, the will of constructive overcoming, the will to freedom: the first element of the aesthetic process.

B. *Art as re-creation*

Re-production is a new forming of reality and itself a reality: the reality of art. A man's portrait is not the man himself but his artistic re-creation. It is a man re-born in the subjective creativity of the imaginative artist, even if it happens to be the self-portrait of the artist himself. So is a sound of nature incorporated into a musical harmony and so the sorrows of life reflected as the mood of a poem.

Nature dissolves in the aesthetical re-creation and becomes art. Art is a re-production of reality according to the purposive nature of individual artist. As a process, it is the process of objectifying subjectivity in the clearest sense of creativeness. It is a method of unlimited freedom and as such the freedom of highest degree and greatest form. The creative genius is therefore the freest and consequently the liveliest of all. The artist re-produces reality to escape reality; be it metaphysical, natural or social.

A Persian Journal of aesthetics continuously prints a classical statement as a philosophical slogan on its cover: "We escape to art so that we do not die from truth."[9]

This is a manifest reaction to a politically motivated social environment in which all social and individual variations of freedom are severely suppressed and the reality of life is a reality of revolting sorrows. The artistic consciousness which is well aware of the situation through varieties of art productions is developing this creative sorrow to the point of a social re-creation of reality. Thus in such a situation the song of life becomes a song of revolution and artistic consciousness, following the inspiration of social life, aims at a revolutionary re-creation of the society.

C. Art as elevation

The aesthetic movement of creativity is a movement from a naturally or socially given reality to an artistically conceived reality. It is at the same time real and ideal movement. It is real because it starts from the reality which it aims to surpass. It is ideal because it departs from a lower form of reality and aims at a higher one. Yet it departs from reality only in order to rejoin it at an aesthetically higher level.

The aesthetic movement of life is therefore a movement

---

[9] The Journal is called "Anahita" which started its publication in 1953 and during the period of political terror by the Shah.

of ideal reality or real ideality. It is ideal but not idealistic. It observes the "drama" of life from the viewpoint of man but not from the viewpoint of God. It makes a god out of man and not a man out of God. As an ideal process it goes beyond life but it stays with life. It reproduces reality and consequently it elevates life.

✶ ✶ ✶

The whole "drama" of human history is the story of a continuous aesthetic movement: overcoming, re-production and elevation. In this endless process of creativity, humanity functions as an organic cultural whole of which science is the brain and art is the heart. They together represent the human will for infinite creativity. Philosophy is the consciousness of this creativity and as such the consciousness of life in its endless continuity. It relates to science and it relates to art. And it reflects the harmony of their functions in dealing with the problem of the "human drama."

Truly speaking the "drama" is but a drama of problems: problems in growth and problems in decline, and life in its perpetual excitement of continuous re-creation. Take these problems away and you shall lose the excitement of their confrontation and overcoming. You shall lose art and you shall lose science.

Freedom from anxiety of life is a necessity, a desire, a means and at the same time an end. Eliminate anxiety from the drama of life and freedom is no longer a desire nor is it a necessity, nor is it a means, nor is it an end.

Life is sadness and the happiness of overcoming sadness. Living is "suffering" and "the excitement" of making suffering suffer and life continue. Life is the continuity of bitter reality and man's unconquerable will of re-creating reality. Life is the infinity of pain leading to the infinity of joy by the re-productive genius of man's mind. Life is the pleasure of living: *creativeness.*

VII

Man and the Endless Universe

"Outwardly we are ruled by these stars, but our inward
nature has become the ruler of the skies, therefore, while in
form thou art the microcosm, in reality thou art the macro-
cosm."

Rumi[1]

IN THIS AGE of the space-discoveries man seems to be a lost
and insignificant identity. His scientific progress has so far
been a progress in the consciousness of his inadequacy. He
is advanced just enough to be aware of his backwardness.
Science gave him strength just to make him realize how weak
and desperate he is. It gave him some confidence in order to
take all his confidence away!

And here he is now: a finite sinking creature in the im-
personal infinity, a conscious individual in the deep and
limitless sea of unconsciousness. A lost point, a removed
reality and yet a man!

Once he considered his earth the center of reality and
religion taught him that there were seven skies beyond his
earth.[2] And it was there in the seven-story building of the
sky that his God resided. Once he had a date with this God

---

[1] Nicholson, R. A. *Selections From Rumi* London, 1950, p. 124.
p. 124.
[2] Reference to an Islamic tradition.

and climbed a mountain to see him.[3] Beneath his flat earth was the seven-story hell; the so called underworld of which religion had warned him. He had two directions to move: up or down, heaven or hell. And he was in between. As proud and stubborn as he was, he did not wish to go down. He wanted to move upward and he could not. Yet the "unreachable" was not too far, it was farther than the mountain top, but no too much farther anyway, one might have reached it, if one could have flown. But man could not fly.

Now the space ship takes him up and moves him around with the speed of some 25,000 miles an hour. And the unreachable remains still unreachable. Not only that, the unreachable moves with him and away from him and faster than him. It is as if the space ship does not move at all, or as if it moves backward, or downward, or in a negative direction.

Man is inadequate and his science teaches him about his inadequacy. He learns about the speed of light of 300,000 kilometers per second just to realize his slowness. He wishes to travel as fast as light and science reminds him of its impossibility. He might be more optimistic than his science and hope for a future when this impossibility becomes a possibility and he can then move as fast as light. And he questions himself: "How far can I travel then?" Not too far! Even if he can spend a million light years of traveling, he can only reach a planet which is just a million light years away. And this is no achievement. This distance brings him to no end, the hope is less than ever. Once man wondered questioning: "Where is the end?" Now he asks himself: "Is there an end?"

Karl Jaspers believes that the wondering man is impelled towards the Infinite:

> "As we move towards the horizon in the world of space without ever reaching it, because the horizon moves with us and re-

---

[3] The story of Moses as described in the *Old Testament*.

establishes itself anew as the encompassing at each moment, so objective research moves towards totalities at each moment which never becomes total and real Being, but must be passed through towards new vistas. Only if all horizons met in one closed whole, so that they formed a finite multiplicity, could we attain, by moving through all the horizons, the one closed Being. Being, however, is not closed for us and the horizons are not finite. On all sides we are impelled towards the Infinite."[4]

And history has seen man's perpetual longing for this unreachable horizon, this undiscovered Infinite, this endless universe.

For a long time the endlessness of the universe had its objective manifestation as the endless space. Now the concept of the endless space is supplemented by the notion of the endless time as its scientific co-relative: time as the fourth dimension! Length, width and height had symbolized an infinite expansion. Time is to signify an infinite extension. The outcome is "infinity in infinity" or the endless extension of the endless expansion. Where is our little man? The little man of few feet and the little life of few years as compared to billions of billion years of light distances in a universe whose most recent development has taken only about five billion years so far![5] What is he more than a lost insignificant identity; lost in the space and lost in time?

II

The wondering man questions himself again: "What am I?" And in this point a search in the space leads to a search in self. An outward wondering develops into an inward re-

---

[4] Kaufmann, Walter. *Existentialism From Dostoevsky to Sartre.* New York: Meridian Books, 1968, p. 149.

[5] Gamow, George. *The Creation of the Universe.* New York: Bantam Books, 1961, p. 135.

flection. The problem then becomes a problem of identity and self-alienation.

Religion identifies man with the supernatural infinite and considers him as a timely stranger whose longing for eternity shall ultimately lead him to eternity. And specifies "To Him we shall return."[6]

This religious slogan is also a first principle of the mystic idealism which advocates the metaphysical unity of all being, thus eliminating the concept of all dualities and pluralities. But the elimination or replacement of a "concept" is not necessarily the elimination or replacement of reality. The notion of an imagined unity does not express reality. Reality is plurality.

The alleged metaphysical unity of all being, derived from a unitary source, be it the religious God or the mystic cosmic spirit, be it He or be it It, is a sign of a psychological desperation. Mysticism and religion, in spite of their linguistic differences, have one and the same psychological foundation. They are both concerned with the problem of human "inadequacy," they both try to relate the limited individual to something limitless; to the endless universe as the unknown infinite. They try to save the desperate individual from his limitations by uniting him with something higher than himself and other than himself. Man becomes a part of cosmic totality in order to save himself from death and destruction.

The basic element of such an artificial identification however is "fear." Fear leads the weak party to join the stronger one. This identification is a relief, yet it is an illusion, a self-deceptive alienation, a desperate resignation of manhood by man in his weakest state of individuality. It is a reduction of man to "It"!

Alan Watts, a modern interpreter of Hindu Mysticism, is a loud speaker of this degrading reduction. He is a thinking

---

6 Islamic slogan.

individual whose thoughts practically deny individuality and thinking. He is a self denial. To him everything is "It," and man is It, and the universe is It. Man becomes "It" in order to last, and this is the psychological weakness, the fear which has haunted Alan Watts' mind. In *The Book* he quotes the following passage from James Broughton:

> "This is It
> and I am It
> and you are It
> and so is That
> and he is It
> and she is It
> and It is It
> and That is That."[7]

Accordingly the "It" which is everything must also be "man." Man as man is limited and finite, while man as It, is unlimited and infinite. He as It includes everything and everything includes him. His death is therefore only a version of this general inclusion. He still lives with It and as It. And my question is: how can man be It and man? If he is It, then he must be a *thing,* but how can we consider man as "thing" and then as "man"?

Can we reduce "manhood" to "thinghood"? The mystic man of everlastingness is an everlasting "thing" who has lost his identity in order to last.

III

The mystic or religious solution to man's problem of identity brings him to a dead end alley of self-alienation. Such a solution is therefore itself a problem by degenerating man's conscious being to a being other than himself. And all this to make this finite being an infinite status!!

Contrary to the demands of the mystics and religionists

7 Watts, Alan, *The Book*. New York: Collier Books, 1967, p. 145.

however, one would not sacrifice identity for infinity. It we consider the man-universe problem as an existential dilemma we may easily avoid the traps of mystical and religious alienation.

First we are to remember that the question of infinity like any other question is a question of conscious life. In other words it is the conscious being who questions. We call this conscious being man, the so called "inadequate man" of consciousness who knows his inadequacy. Eliminate his consciousness and the problem no longer exists. Infinity is no more a problem nor is it a reality. The universe is no longer *endless* nor is it universe. Science is then of no use. The space ship has no longer an aim, it is lost and this time no one knows that it is lost. The discovery is lost because the discoverer is lost and with him the consciousness of the discovery. The endless universe and the endless time are no longer of any use nor of any meaning. They would die with the conscious life if the conscious living dies.

Conscious life is true existence. It is superior to any other life. It is that portion of the universe which is superior to the universe as a whole. It is a part of the whole for which the whole exists and because of which the whole has meaning. Thus the conscious life does not exist for the universe but the universe for the conscious life. Who is to conceive infinity, who is to think about endlessness if the thinking and conceiving man is eliminated? Who would consider the preserved universe of everlastingness if the consciousness of being as the being of consciousness is lost, if man is gone?

The universe is great, endless and eternal, but it does not know it, the man is small, inadequate and perishing, but he knows it. The sun of our galaxy according to scientific predictions shall receive its death award 5,000,000,000 years from now,[8] but it does not know it; a revolutionist with a

---

[8] Gamow. *Op cit.*, p. 16.

fatal wound shall die in a few seconds, but he knows it. He reaches death with an awareness of life. And this is the main difference between man and the sun! Man feels life and sun does not. Man knows that he is not the sun, but the sun does not know that it is the sun. Man is conscious of his identity, but any other part of the universe is not. Man is different from nature and truly he is his difference with nature. He is the thinking nature. He is not a senseless generality of endlessness but a senseful particularity of existential limitations.

But man as "limitation" is a limited outwardness only. He is unrestricted inwardness. He is inner freedom and he knows that. The endlessness of his soul is the endlessness of his freedom. A freedom of which he is aware and because of which he precisely knows what he is and what he is not; that he is "he" and he is not "it"; that he is one and not the other, not everyone, not every other one!

According to those astrophysicists who consider the universe as the pattern of a never ending "steady state," similarity and sameness is the essential characteristic of cosmic reality. All galaxies look alike and none of them are different from ours. No matter what direction we look and how far our observations develop in the space, we find a basic similarity everywhere: space is the same and planets are the same. And not only a search in the space, but also a search in time would lead us to the same "sameness"! Hence according to the theory of "relativity" time as fourth dimension of cosmic realities, is the co-relative of space. According to the terminology of George Gamow:

> "The behavior of the universe in time must be the same as its behavior in space."[9]

Thus looking forward or backward in time, or in space we observe the same basic things: similar galaxies! And we may then conceive of galaxies in formation, in development

---

[9] *Ibid.,* p. 30.

and in decay. Birth and death following each other constantly and continuously! And matter constantly preserved and with it the material universe of infinity: the infinity of "sameness"!

The finite man of conscious life is a different story. He represents a finite life yet an infinity of conscious choices and colorful "variations." The source of this conscious variability is man's freedom without which his life is no life. Every man is a different man and as such a different universe: a universe of creative choice! Stars are not persons and are the same. Men are persons and are different. Personality as the attitude of consciousness is the meaningful variation—a variation which can best be known as the function of freedom. This is an adequate explanation of the fact that men are free and stars are not.

The next point is that this conscious life is itself endless. Man who wishes to discover the endless universe is himself an endless discovery. He has not been able to conquer the universe, but the universe has not been able to conquer him either. Yet man has a hope and the senseless universe has none. The universe is more inadequate than man. Man is aware of his inadequacies and the universe as a whole is not.

Rumi calls man's inward nature "the ruler of the skies," and believes that man is only outwardly governed by cosmic forces. Here Rumi, although a mystic, explains an existential reality: the dynamic force of consciousness. Consciousness as the sole manifestation of man's inward reality is free and endless, or endlessly free.

As far as Rumi stresses man's inward freedom, he echoes an existential conception. Yet this is not his entire position. His ultimate concern is the mystic unity. He liberates the conscious individual from the unconscious nature but leads him to the trap of the mystical resignation where all pluralities dissolve into a cosmic unity. Rumi's position is therefore twofold. He moves from nature to conscious existence and from the conscious existence to the supernatural. To me

Rumi's significance however lies in the first move: the emancipation of the individual as self-reflective consciousness.

Goethe re-echoes the voice of Rumi when he says "Ich kehre in mich selbst Züruck und Finde eine Welt."[10] (I return to myself and there I find a world.) It is in this inner reality that man himself is a universe, free from the deterministic laws of causation which govern the external world. While the inner-universe of man is a universe of freedom, the external universe is dominated by rules and regulations concerning every movement, every function and every development. And a Newton, a conscious reality of finite state was to discover for this senseless infinity, how it moves and how it functions. I would call this inward reality of consciousness, this Newton, in spite of his physical size and short-lasting life, superior to that external huge and senseless reality which even does not know that it is a reality, which moves but does not know how, which functions but does not understand why.

---

[10] Goethe, Wolfgang. *Das Leiden des Jungen-Werthers.*

Index

Albrecht, Franz 65
Aquinas, Thomas 46
Chopin 64, 65
Darwin, Charles 67
Descartes, René 21
Dewey, John 31
Dilthey, Wilhelm 74, 75
Eisenhower, D. D. 36
Erkel, Ferenc 65, 66
Ferguson, Wallace K. 75
Feuerbach, L. A. 50
Galileo 30
Gamow, George 85
Goethe, Johann Wolfgang 87
Hegel, G. W. F. 11, 17, 31, 40, 48, 49
Homer 45, 47
Jaspers, Karl 80
Justinian 45
Kant, Immanuel 11, 60, 61, 62, 63

Lenin, Vladimir Ilych 58, 59, 63
Lowell, James 20
Lieber, Hans-Joachim 5
MacIver, Robert 25
Marx, Karl 27, 34, 49, 50, 58, 59 60
Moses 47, 48
Mueller, Gustav 24
Newton, Isaac 87, 90
Nietzsche, Friedrich 15, 50, 51, 52, 67, 68, 72
Plato 21, 57, 58, 59
Rembrandt 64
Rumi, Jalalledin 79, 86, 87
Schelling, F. W. J. 71, 72, 73, 74
Spinoza, Benedict 46, 47, 48
Stalin, Joseph 65
Wagner, Richard 67, 68
Zeus 57